Country Living

COUNTRY CATS

Country Living

COUNTRY CATS

Adventures from Kitchen to Haystack—
The Busy Days of a Cat's Life

Permissions and acknowledgments appear on Pages 94–95.

Recognizing the importance of preserving what has been written, it is the policy of William Morrow and Company, Inc., and its imprints and affiliates to have the books it publishes printed on acid-free paper, and we exert our best efforts to that end.

Library of Congress Cataloging-in-Publication Data

Country living country cats.—1st ed.
          p.   cm.
     ISBN 0-688-11182-3
     1. Cats—Miscellanea.   2. Cats—Pictorial works.
  I. Title: Country cats.
  SF445.5.C67   1992
  636.8′088′7—dc20   91-39961
                                                          CIP

Printed in Singapore

First Edition
1   2   3   4   5   6   7   8   9   10

COUNTRY LIVING STAFF

Rachel Newman, Editor
Jason Kontos, Executive Editor
Nina Williams, Editor at Large

Designed by Barbara Scott-Goodman
Edited by Shannon Rothenberger
Produced by Smallwood and Stewart, Inc., New York City

A Cat's Prayer

When upon your book I walk,
As you're reading, do not squawk.
Read instead my tail, my fur,
Harken to my throaty purr,
Gaze into my moonlit eyes;
It won't take long to recognise
That instead of drearsome reading,
It's the cat you should be feeding.

INTRODUCTION
For Leo

I always thought of myself as a dog lover until Leo, an orange cat, entered my life. I inherited him years ago when I moved into a home in the country. The departing owners, unable to take him along, asked if I could adopt him and, with trepidation, I did.

I always thought of cats as unresponsive and dull creatures that mostly sat around like meat loaves. But Leo changed all that. From the beginning, he made it perfectly clear that I had been allowed to move into *his* home. He appropriated a position on the sofa and that became his throne. Leo had a routine and it was my obligation to accommodate myself to his schedule. He let me know the time of day he preferred to go out, and when he liked to come in. I researched his food likes and dislikes and came up with precisely what he wanted or else: the cold shoulder.

I came to realize that the more I catered to his every whim, the sweeter he would be to me. Joyous was the day Leo allowed me to mother him! And mother him I did. I worried when he was out in the cold. I fretted if I had to work late and couldn't make his favorite feeding time. The day a raccoon chased him up a tree, I was ready to call the Fire Department, the Police, and the F.B.I.

Yes, Leo became a person to me...and he taught me that cats, like people, can be spirited, idiosyncratic, eccentric, dignified, silly, coy, precocious, curious, ornery, and utterly and completely lovable.

Rachel Newman
Editor in Chief

C ats sleep

an average of

eighteen hours a day.

In America, the cat is the most popular house pet, surpassing the canary, the goldfish, and, yes, even the dog. In fact, cats outnumber dogs by more than five million.

The polite cat does not always respond. He gives you time to reconsider.

CAT BREEDS

Purebreds account for half the kittens in the United States. There are more than two dozen registered breeds of cat; the three oldest are the Persian, the Manx, and the Siamese. The most popular:

Abyssinian: The Abyssinian and the related longhair Somali are unique in the cat-breeding world due to their agouti—or grizzled—coat, which is a rich, coppery red with dark ticking and stripes down the backbone, legs, and flanks. Like the Siamese, the Abyssinian has a long, lean body.

American Shorthair: The American Shorthair is the best-known breed of cat and is often called an alley cat. These stocky, round-headed descendants of working cats come in all colors and have the even temperament ideal for family life.

Balinese: The Balinese has the same build and coloring as the Siamese, but its coat is long and silky. Like the Siamese, it is acrobatic and, occasionally, aloof.

Birman: A long-bodied, short-legged cat with an Angora-type coat and Himalayan color points, the Birman always has white feet.

Bombay: A shiny black hybrid of the Burmese and the American Shorthair, the Bombay is called "the cat with the patent leather coat and the copper penny eyes."

British Shorthair: Very much like the American Shorthair, the British Shorthair is more massive and has a thicker coat.

Burmese: The Burmese is a solidly built cat with a very short, sleek, sable coat. It is known for its rich, golden eye color.

Chartreux: Originally from France, the Chartreux is a stocky, blue-coat shorthair with a silvery sheen. It is slightly larger than the American and European Shorthairs.

Egyptian Mau: This breed is distinguished by leopard-like spots in a silver or bronze tabby pattern. In shows, great importance is given to the Mau's forehead markings and "mascara" lines on its cheeks.

Havana Brown: The Havana Brown is named after the chestnut brown cigar color it exhibits. This shorthair has oval green eyes.

Himalayan: Also called Colorpoint Longhairs, these are Siamese-patterned cats with Persian-type bodies. They have as many color variations as the Siamese, from seal point to flame, and can also be solid coated. Generally, they are more active than Persians and calmer than Siamese.

Japanese Bobtail: The ancient good luck symbol of Japan, the Japanese Bobtail is a slender, stub-tailed cat with short hair and calico coloring.

Korat: From Thailand, this quiet-voiced, gentle cat has a heart-shaped face and large green eyes. Its silver-blue coat was described in an old Thai poem as having "roots like clouds and tips like silver."

Maine Coon: The Maine Coon is a large, muscular cat with shaggy tabby fur and tufted cheeks. Related to the Norwegian Forest Cat, it is hardy and independent.

Manx: Once unique to the Isle of Man, the playful Manx is bred for taillessness. A short-haired, varicolored cat, it is small and rounded, with an arched back and long hind legs.

Persian: The Persian is the most popular breed. There are fourteen types; all are stocky and short legged with round heads, small ears, and flat faces. Their long, silky fur comes in a profusion of colors. Angoras have been so commonly crossed with Persians that they are now in this category. Of them all, blue-eyed whitehairs seem to be the favorite.

Ragdoll: Related to the Birman and White Persian, the Ragdoll resembles both. Its name comes from its extreme docility and rumored inability to respond to pain, feel fear, or fight other animals. Because of its passive nature, the Ragdoll is not recommended for children or outdoors.

Rex: The Rex has short, crimped hair like a Persian lamb, curly whiskers, a long, straight nose, and a whippy tail. It is intelligent, affectionate, and nonshedding, but sensitive to cold.

Russian Blue: Even bluer than the Korat, the Russian Blue is extremely lithe. Its coat is more plush than that of any other cat. It has been called Archangel because of its slender grace.

Scottish Fold: The lop ears of the Scottish Fold are small and folded over its forehead like a cap, giving it a wide-eyed look of surprise or a sad look, which is not necessarily an indication of its inner feelings.

Siamese: These popular, elegant cats have pale bodies with darker color points and blue eyes. The markings appear in shades from the almost black seal point to palest lilac point, on coats ranging from fawn to arctic white. They are prized for their elongated heads and svelte bodies. Siamese are known for having exuberant personalities in every way. This cat is the most likely to learn tricks.

If your cat is	His age in human years is
1	15
2	25
4	40
7	50
10	60
15	75
20	105
30	120

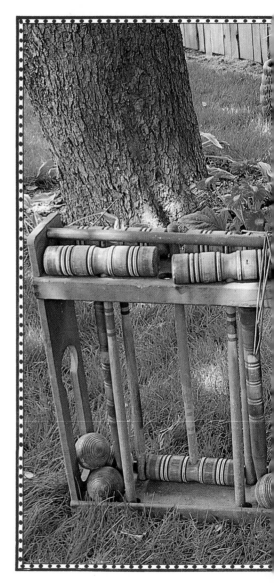

A well-bred cat never flinches. When startled, a bored expression is appropriate.

∘∙∘∙∘∙∘∙∘∙

The polite cat will interrupt your phone conversations. After all, if you are speaking and no one else is present, any decent cat will respond as if you are addressing her. She wouldn't want you to get a reputation for talking to yourself.

∘∙∘∙∘∙∘∙∘∙

The established way for a cat to defuse any awkward social situation is to groom himself.

If there is a new cat in the house, it is usual for the veteran country cat to lavish her owner with increased offerings from the field in hopes that her services will not be forgotten. The wise recipient will show the proper enthusiasm.

The refined cat does not waste words. She conveys her distaste with the slight shake of a paw, as if it were wet.

Clowder is the correct term for a group of cats.

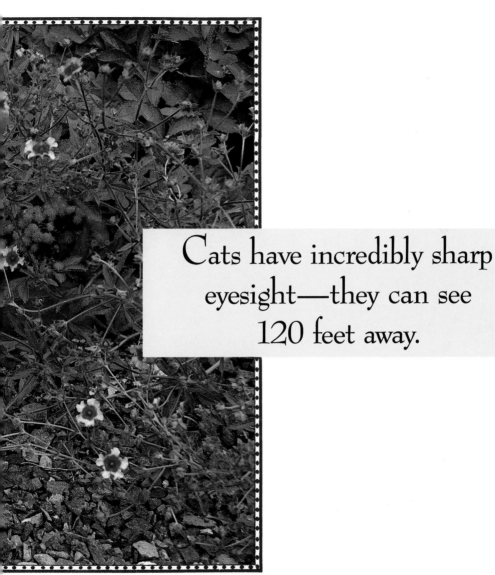

Cats have incredibly sharp
eyesight—they can see
120 feet away.

Felix the Cat was the first kitty cartoon star. Other popular cartoon cats are Tom (of Tom and Jerry), Krazy Kat, Percy the Cat, Sylvester (who was always thwarted by 'Tweetie Pie), Courageous Cat, and the Pink Panther. Top Cat was the cartoon star of 60s television. Tom and Jerry, the cat-and-mouse act, broke from cartoons to dance with Gene Kelly in *Anchors Aweigh* and swim with Esther Williams in *Dangerous When Wet*. Altogether, they won seven Oscars, including one in 1943 for *Yankee Doodle Mouse*.

Cats prefer
to walk on
the sunny side
of the street.

When among cats, one must remember that they do not shake hands. Requests of "Gimme yer paw" will result in a withering stare. As a matter of fact, touching a cat's paw at all is taboo. The correct cat greeting is the side approach and sly shoulder rub. Continue on without a backward glance.

A roundabout course,
with frequent stops, is
the wisest. A proper cat
never rushes to her goal.

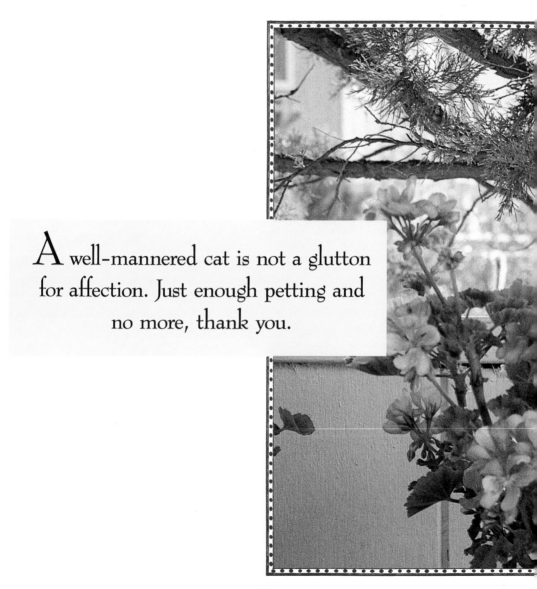

A well-mannered cat is not a glutton for affection. Just enough petting and no more, thank you.

Edward Lear, the Victorian author of "The Owl and the Pussycat," so loved his tabby Foss that when he moved, he insisted that his new house be built as an exact replica of his old one, so as not to confuse the cat.

When the cat's

away . . .

It is necessary to

keep plenty of cat

accessories around to

remind the mice who

really owns the house.

Unlike some creatures, the cat is not a pack animal. He prefers the pleasure of his own company.

Famous literary cat lovers are Victor Hugo, Sir Walter Scott, The Brontës, Charles Dickens (whose cat would snuff his candle because she was so jealous of his work), William Wordsworth, Edgar Allan Poe, Henry James (who wrote with a cat on his shoulder), Mark Twain, and Ernest Hemingway (who at one time had thirty cats).

Cats have long given up on teaching manners to dogs, though on the special occasions when they do (conditionally) enjoy canine company, cats try to set the good example.

One of the cat's most endearing qualities is his curiosity, which often leads to mischief. But when Harvey, an English kitten, was found in his owner's washing machine, he was already ten minutes through the cycle. Wiser and cleaner, Harvey was fluffed with a hair dryer and returned to sit in front of the machine to watch the clothes go round.

It is important to refrain from telling a cat, even in jest, to "Get a job." A cat's job is already very difficult. Every morning, she must rise at six to begin diplomatically convincing a reluctant creature many times her size to wake up and make her breakfast. After such an accomplishment, she deserves her rest.

One of the treats cats enjoy best is the herb catnip. A member of the mint family, catnip is easy to grow in the garden or a pot. Its leaves, fresh or dried, will cause kitty to purr contentedly, loll happily about, and generally have a very good time.

The game Cat's Cradle evolved from an Eastern European custom of rocking a cat in a cradle in the house of newlyweds to guarantee an immediate pregnancy for the bride.

C ats are known for their independence, but the State of Illinois nonetheless once tried to pass a law to prevent them from chasing birds. Governor Adlai Stevenson promptly vetoed the bill. "The problem of cat versus bird is as old as time," he wrote. "If we attempt to resolve it by legislation, who knows but what we may be called upon to take sides as well in the age-old problems of dog versus cat, bird versus bird, or even bird versus worm."

If it looks like "something the cat dragged in," it probably is. Furthermore, custom dictates that the cat of the house be consulted before the object is thrown away.

Cat Etiquette requires that a cat keep a serene expression and refrain from vulgar displays of emotion. Hence, the expression, "That's enough to make a cat laugh."

When a kitten drinks water, she swallows only once for every four or five laps she takes. And to a cat, a can of cat food is the equivalent of four or five fat mice.

A cat decides if food
is acceptable or not
from a distance
of three feet.

True, the purr signifies a cat's approval, but it originates as a homing signal the mother cat uses to call her young ones. The kittens remember the particular vibrations they felt when they fed.

Texas, where they do everything big, is home to the most prolific cat on record. Dusty, a tabby, has given birth to 420 kittens. The oldest first-time mother: Smitty, a retired rat catcher in England, who gave birth to one perfect kitten at the age of 28.

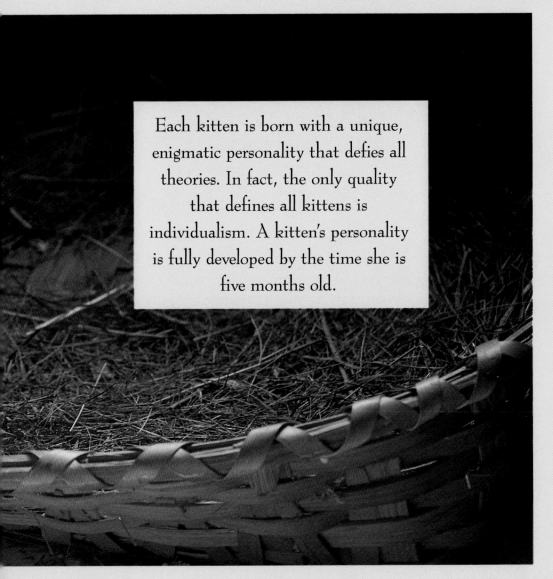

Each kitten is born with a unique, enigmatic personality that defies all theories. In fact, the only quality that defines all kittens is individualism. A kitten's personality is fully developed by the time she is five months old.

A cat learns his own name quickly, especially if he is being called to dinner. Less important occasions do not require an RSVP.

Cat games are based on the mock assault, from play fighting to the "mouse pounce," the "bird swat," and the "fish scoop." The best kitty toys are very light, so they can be tossed about easily, and very soft, so teeth and claws can sink satisfyingly into them. Simple household objects are more fun for cats than expensive cat toys.

Not many sounds escape a cat, but his hearing is highly selective, to say the least.

According to Cat Etiquette, one can never be too clean or too well rested.

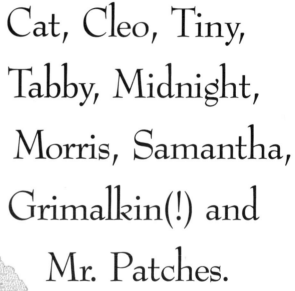

The ten most common names for cats: Fog, Cat, Cleo, Tiny, Tabby, Midnight, Morris, Samantha, Grimalkin(!) and Mr. Patches.

According to the Institute for the Study of Animal Problems in Washington, DC, cats and dogs are either right-"handed" or left-"handed," preferring to use either their right or left paws.

There is actually no need to build a Cat House, as cats prefer to squeeze into small, useful spaces around the home. Cats suggest finding another place for the apples and the mail. It is also advisable to check the kitchen cupboards for Felix before closing the doors.

It has been suggested that cats cannot see themselves in mirrors because they are so completely immersed in being cats, and so good at it, that they can not imagine being anywhere else.

Despite the phrase "the cat's pyjamas," preferred gifts for a cat are food, toys, and catnip.

Cat lovers often leave money to their pets. In the 1960s, the world's richest cats lived in California (of course): Brownie and Hellcat were left $415,000. But legacies to pets do not get special treatment from the government. In fact, one cat who inherited $7,000 got a Notice of Taxes Due for $600 from the I.R.S.

It took a genius like Sir Isaac Newton to invent the cat door, so don't be embarrassed if you don't have one. Here, the cat of the house indicates the proper location for the cat door, and waits patiently for its installation.

Given their celebrated curiosity, cats
love adventure. This is true of one four-
month-old kitten in Switzerland—she
followed a group of climbers all the way
to the top of the 14,691 foot Matterhorn
in the Alps.

It is a cat's prerogative to change her mind.

PHOTOGRAPHY CREDITS

42–43	Keith Scott Morton	70–71	Jessie Walker
45	Keith Scott Morton	72	Jessie Walker
46–47	Jessie Walker	74–75	Keith Scott Morton
48	Paul Kopelow	76–77	Keith Scott Morton
51	Lynn Karlin	80–81	Keith Scott Morton
52–53	Keith Scott Morton	82–83	Jessie Walker
54	Paul Kopelow	84	Jessie Walker
57	Michael Dunne	86–87	Ben Rosenthal
58–59	Lynn Karlin	88	Rick Patrick
60–61	Lynn Karlin	91	Keith Scott Morton
63	Keith Scott Morton	92–93	Lynn Karlin
64	Lynn Karlin	94	Keith Scott Morton
66–67	Lynn Karlin	95	Lynn Karlin
68–69	Lynn Karlin	96	Lynn Karlin